THE
PERSIAN
EMPIRE

*W*ith special thanks to Megan Cifarelli,
Norbert Schimmel Fellow in the Art of the Mediterranean
at The Metropolitan Museum of Art, New York City,
for her invaluable assistance in
reading the manuscript.

CULTURES OF THE PAST

THE
PERSIAN
EMPIRE

KAREN ZEINERT

BENCHMARK BOOKS

MARSHALL CAVENDISH
NEW YORK

To Wendy

Benchmark Books
Marshall Cavendish Corporation
99 White Plains Road
Tarrytown, New York 10591-9001

Library of Congress Cataloging-in-Publication Data
Zeinert, Karen.
   The Persian Empire / by Karen Zeinert.
      p.   cm. — (Cultures of the past)
   Includes bibliographical references (p.   ) and index.
Summary: Traces the rise and fall of the Persian Empire from its earliest days to the
seventh century, when it was conquered by the Arabs. The culture, artistic achieve-
ments, religion, and legacy of the once mighty empire are discussed.
   ISBN 0-7614-0089-3 (lib. bdg.)
   1. Achaemenid dynasty, 559–330 B.C.—Juvenile literature. 2. Iran—
History—To 640—Juvenile literature. [1. Iran—History—To 640.] I. Title.
II. Series.
   DS281.Z45   1997
   935'.05—dc20   95-44123

Printed in Hong Kong

Book design by Carol Matsuyama
Photo research by Barbara Scott

Front cover: The ancient Persian "Parthian shot" depicted in a later Islamic miniature painting from the Topkapi Palace Museum, Istanbul, Turkey
Back cover: Glazed brick panel of protective spirit, from the Palace of Darius, Susa,
late sixth–early fifth century B.C.E.

Photo Credits
Front cover: courtesy of Giraudon/Art Resource, NY; back cover: courtesy of Erich
Lessing/Art Resource, NY; page 6: The Metropolitan Museum of Art, Fletcher
Fund, 1954, 54.3.3; pages 7, 8, 30, 66: Robert Harding/Picture Library; pages 10,
17, 25, 26, 63: Giraudon/Art Resource, NY; pages 13, 28–29, 32, 56, 59: SEF/Art
Resource, NY; pages 15, 20, 37: Erich Lessing/Art Resource, NY; page 21: The
Metropolitan Museum of Art, Fletcher Fund, 1934, 34.33; pages 31, 45, 48: ©British
Museum; page 34: W. Hillie/Leo de Wys Inc., NY; page 35: The Metropolitan
Museum of Art, Fletcher Fund, 1965, 65.126; pages 36, 42: Louvre ©PHOTO
R.M.N.; page 38: Topkapi Sarayi Palace Museum, Istanbul, Turkey; page 40: Yale
University Art Gallery; page 44: Edinburgh University Library E.U.L. Or. Ms. 161,
f. 48v; page 49: The Cleveland Museum of Art, Leonard C. Hanna, Jr., Fund, 64.96;
pages 51, 54: Jehangir Gazdar/Woodfin Camp & Associates; page 60: Zeynep
Sumen/Tony Stone Worldwide; page 64: The Metropolitan Museum of Art, Gift of
Arthur A. Houghton, Jr., 1970, 1970.301.2, folio 22v; page 67: Alan & Linda
Detrick/Photo Researchers, Inc.; page 68: Art Resource, NY; page 71: Nimatallah/
Art Resource

CONTENTS

CHAPTER ONE

THE FIRST WORLD EMPIRE

In 330 B.C.E.*, Alexander the Great of Macedonia, a powerful military leader, stared in awe at his latest prize, Persepolis (per-SEP-uh-lus), one of the capitals of the Persian Empire. Even though he had heard many stories about this great city, he still was not prepared for the beauty and incredible luxury he saw. He marveled at the huge buildings with gold-rimmed roofs. As he explored them he gazed in wonder at the elaborately painted wall sculptures, decorated with hundreds of precious gems. But Alexander's biggest surprise came when he learned what was stored in the royal treasury building. Here he found 270 tons of gold coins and 1,000 tons of silver bars.

While the conqueror was packing up his spoils of war—it took ten thousand horses and five thousand camels just to carry off the royal treasury—Alexander's troops raced after the fleeing Persian king, Darius III. Before they could reach the king, however, Darius's own bodyguards killed him. The guards were enraged at the king's loss on the battlefield, for it had cost the Persians their empire—an empire with a proud past.

This gold drinking vessel shaped like a lion probably belonged to the royal courts of one of the Achaemenid Persian kings. These kings were known as fierce warriors who surrounded themselves with beauty and luxury when they were at home.

*Many systems of dating have been used by different cultures throughout history. This series of books uses B.C.E. (Before Common Era) and C.E. (Common Era) instead of B.C. (Before Christ) and A.D. (Anno Domini) out of respect for the diversity of the world's peoples.

The First Persians

About fifteen hundred years before Alexander, a seminomadic tribe left the region around the northern part of the Caspian Sea and began moving onto a vast plateau in what is now Iran. Some think these were the first Persians. Tall mountains surrounded the plateau, many of the peaks more than two miles high. Deserts

Persepolis was the most magnificent of all the Persian capitals. The most powerful animals in the ancient world, the lion and the bull, battle on this relief sculpture that decorated a Persian palace. The carved image of these animals was probably originally painted.

7

covered most of the center of the plateau. These deserts were very cold in winter and so hot in summer that snakes and lizards risked being burned to death if they stayed in the sun for more than a few minutes. Although most of the area could barely support herders and their families, the valleys in the southern part of the plateau were more fertile. Eventually the tribe, known as the Aryans, settled there, in an area now called Fars. The Greeks called it Pars, and it is from them that we get the name Persia. (In 1935, Persia changed its name to Iran, after its founders, the Aryans.)

The Persians were not alone on the plateau. To the north of

Even some of the valleys of Fars suffer from harsh growing conditions, and only hardy crops can be grown. The olive trees shown here produce a rich oil that can be traded, used in cooking, and even burned as a fuel for lamps.

Fars was Elam (EE-lahm), an ancient country whose leaders were experienced in running government and winning wars. The Persians had numerous contacts with the Elamites, and the newcomers adopted many ideas from the old civilization.

Another nation that occupied a place on the plateau was Media. This country had a strong army, and it eventually took control of Fars. As was the custom then, the ruler of a defeated tribe or nation might retain his crown if he swore obedience to his conqueror. The king of Fars agreed to do this, and his family, the Achaemenians (AK-uh-MEEN-ee-ans), continued to rule their kingdom.

King Cyrus's Triumphs

By 600 B.C.E. the Achaemenians and the people they ruled were growing in number, strength, and skills. The king of Media was deeply concerned about this situation, for he saw the possibility of a revolt. He tried to head off trouble by marrying his daughter to a noble in the Achaemenian family. Their son became known in history as Cyrus the Great, and he inherited the Achaemenian throne about 560 B.C.E.

Cyrus resented being ruled by a Median king, even if it was his grandfather. A Greek historian, who wrote many years later, tells us what happened next. Cyrus was making plans to free Fars when he was approached by Harpagus, a general in the Median army. Harpagus hated his king—and he had good reason: the Median ruler had killed Harpagus's son to punish the general for not obeying orders. Even worse, the king had cut off the boy's head, put it on a platter, and served the bloody trophy to Harpagus at a banquet. Understandably, the Median general was looking for an opportunity for revenge. Harpagus encouraged Cyrus to attack Media, promising to help the Persians by defecting from the Median army during the battle and bringing most of the army with him.

Cyrus accepted the general's help, and in 550 B.C.E. the Persians attacked and defeated Media. They gained both their independence and Median colonies on the Mediterranean Sea. This was the beginning of the Persian Empire.

The Medes, shown here on a Persian relief sculpture from Persepolis, were one of the most powerful people in ancient Iran. They always appear in Persian art wearing long, heavy trousers and a knee-length tunic with a belt. The round hats may indicate that they are high-ranking ambassadors to the Persian king.

Cyrus's growing power concerned other kings in the region. Did he, they wondered, want more than Media? One of the most troubled kings was Croesus (KREE-sus), the ruler of Lydia (in modern Turkey).

While Croesus worried, Cyrus worked at uniting the Persians and the Medians. The Persian ruler did indeed have his eye on Lydia, but he was unwilling to risk an attack until he had the loyalty of all his subjects. By all accounts, Cyrus was a rare, natural-born ruler. He was a handsome, dashing man, said to be strong, wise, and fair. The Persians loved him, and the Medians quickly grew to respect and admire him. In fact, over the years they would become some of his most loyal subjects.

When Cyrus believed that Persia was ready, he, with help from Harpagus, fought and defeated the Lydians in 547 B.C.E. Cyrus not only gained another country, but he also found untold wealth in the Lydian treasury—enough money to finance his dream of a great Persian Empire. Shortly after, he conquered the ancient kingdom of Babylonia, and with it gained the land stretching to the Mediterranean coast.

The Achaemenians' Vast Realm

Upon Cyrus's death, in 529 B.C.E., his son Cambyses (kam-BY-seez) became king. Cambyses planned to continue to expand the Persian Empire, and he chose Egypt as his next prize. Before attacking, however, the new ruler had to make sure that all his subjects were firmly under control. For the next four years, despite rumors of possible revolts, the empire remained peaceful, and the king planned his invasion of Egypt. When Cambyses did invade, the Egyptians were amazed, for the Persian army had had to cross a hot, barren wasteland—the Sinai Desert. After entering Egypt, the Persians quickly took Memphis, a major city on the Nile River. After capturing the pharaoh, the ruler of Egypt, they forced the Egyptians to surrender.

Cambyses had planned to continue his conquests once he had Egypt under control, but he was not as successful in his next endeavors. Fifty thousand soldiers sent into the desert to capture the Oasis of Ammon died in a fierce sandstorm that literally buried

When Cyrus's army headed toward Lydia in 547 B.C.E., Croesus, the king of Lydia, hoped to stop the Persians once and for all at the city of Pteria (TIR-ee-uh). The battle there, however, was not decisive. But since it was nearly winter, Croesus decided to stop fighting until the following spring, and he ordered his army to return to Sardis. He assumed that Cyrus would retire for the winter as well.

But Cyrus had come 1,200 miles to fight Croesus, and he wasn't willing to return home without conquering the Lydians. So he waited until he was certain that Croesus had reached Sardis and had disbanded his army. Then Cyrus and his army raced toward Sardis, hoping to arrive before Croesus had time to reassemble his troops.

Croesus was stunned when messengers told him that Cyrus was approaching. The Lydian king gathered what few men he could, sent messengers to allies for help, and rode out to fight the Persians.

Encountering fierce warriors, Croesus was forced to retreat to Sardis. This walled city sat on top of a steep-sided plateau, and Croesus thought it was impregnable. The Lydian king had enough supplies to last for a while, and he believed that all he had to do was guard the city's only entry and wait for his allies to arrive.

Meanwhile, Cyrus offered a reward to any man in his army who could figure out how to scale the plateau and invade the city. For almost two weeks the Persians studied the landscape without arriving at a solution. Then, on the thirteenth day, some Persians were watching a Lydian guard walk around the top of the wall. The guard's helmet fell off and rolled partway down the side of the plateau. The Persians stared in disbelief as the guard easily worked his way down the seemingly impossible terrain to retrieve his helmet. They smiled as the man climbed up the cliff to reenter the city. The soldiers noted each move, then reported their discovery to Cyrus. The next morning the Persians scaled the plateau, scrambled over the city's sparsely guarded wall, and forced Croesus to surrender.

them alive. Others, led by Cambyses, captured Nubia, a country south of Egypt, but many soldiers died of starvation on their return to Memphis. Supposedly the soldiers resorted to cannibalism to save some of the troops, and every tenth man was killed and eaten. The third group failed to capture Carthage, a powerful Phoenician (fi-NISH-an) city west of Egypt on the Mediterranean shore of Africa. Phoenician sailors, the majority of the Persian navy, had refused to attack their countrymen.

Some historians believe that the losses Cambyses encountered drove him mad. Greek historians tell us that he became unspeakably cruel. One story has it that he plunged his knife into a bull considered sacred by the Egyptians, murdered his own wife, and shot his son with a bow and arrow.

In 522 B.C.E. a man claiming to be Cambyses's brother declared himself king of Persia. Since he had gained a good deal of support, he was considered to be a real threat. Cambyses made plans to return home to secure his throne, but he died before reaching Persia.

Darius (da-RYE-us), leader of Cambyses's best troops in Egypt, took over. He returned to Persia, threw out the challenger, and pronounced himself king. A number of conquered nations, believing that Darius would be a weak ruler, decided to revolt. Darius wasn't about to let any province go, and he put down nineteen rebellions to prove his point.

Although Darius had a difficult beginning as king, he became one of Persia's greatest rulers. Like Cyrus, he governed wisely, and this earned him the respect and affection of his subjects. He built roads, established a postal system, and standardized weights and measures and coinage.

Darius also began construction on Persia's fifth capital city, Persepolis. Although this was the largest of the capitals, he

Nations from all over the Persian Empire brought tribute, or rich gifts, to the Persian king, allowing him to have a luxurious lifestyle and support his army. These tributaries are from Phoenicia, the powerful seafaring nation on the Mediterranean coast.

continued to use the other four cities as well, traveling to Pasargadae (pah-SAR-gah-dee) for special ceremonies, Babylon and Susa for official business, and Ecbatana (ek-BAT-un-uh) to escape the summer heat.

Darius continued to expand the empire, which further increased its wealth. He marched into India and took control of all the land west of the Indus River. In the spring of 513 B.C.E., he launched the first Asian invasion of Europe, hoping to conquer Greek city-states that had become serious trading rivals.

According to Greek historians, Darius was extremely well prepared for his European invasion. He had seventy thousand soldiers, three hundred ships, and a bridge of boats that stretched across the Strait of Bosporus, which separates Asia from Europe. His troops, it was said, could actually walk across the water to Thrace, a region north of Greece.

THERMOPYLAE

One of the most famous battles in ancient history took place in 480 B.C.E. at Thermopylae, a narrow mountain pass located eighty-five miles northwest of Athens. This site was chosen by the Greek army, made up of 4,000 troops from several city-states. The army hoped to delay the invading Persians until the Greek navy could sink the Persian fleet, forcing the enemy to retreat.

When Xerxes reached the pass, he ordered his men, 180,000 strong, to force their way through the narrow opening. Although the soldiers charged the pass four times, they failed to break through.

A Greek traitor, Ephialtes, then approached Xerxes, offering to show him a little-used path that would allow the Persians to attack the Greeks from behind. Greek soldiers assigned to watch this trail were unable to hold it when the Persians advanced, but the soldiers managed to send a warning to Leonidas, the king of Sparta, who was in charge of the Greek army.

Knowing that all his men would be lost unless they retreated quickly, Leonidas sent all but three hundred handpicked soldiers away. Those who remained delayed the Persians as long as possible, fighting to their deaths, so that the others might reach safety.

Once the Persians defeated the Greeks at Thermopylae, they advanced to Athens, where they set fire to the city. The Greeks never forgave the Persians for the destruction of their beautiful city, and one hundred and fifty years later Alexander the Great destroyed Persepolis in revenge.

Darius encountered little difficulty in Thrace. Serious problems arose, however, as he pushed northward. The Scythians (SITH-ee-anz), a nomadic tribe, had destroyed everything edible in the area, including storehouses and fields of grain. The Persians had been used to living off the land as they advanced, and they could not continue their drive. Nor could they engage and defeat the Scythians, who wisely avoided battle. Darius was eventually forced to retreat. He returned to Persia but left behind enough soldiers in Thrace to hold it and make a drive south into Macedonia, which they took. Persia now held land in Asia, Africa, and Europe, and its empire was at its farthest extent.

Darius's long rule came to a close with his death in 486 B.C.E. His son, Xerxes (ZURK-seez), succeeded him. Xerxes, too, wanted to expand the empire. He set his sights on the Greeks. In

Alexander the Great was a young man when he brought his mighty army to conquer Persia. A romantic figure, Alexander's exploits were celebrated in art for centuries. This portrait of him comes from a mosaic (a picture made of hundreds of tiny stones or tiles) found in Pompeii, Italy, and dates to the third century C.E.

15

the spring of 480 B.C.E., he led a combined land and sea invasion of Greece. The Greeks made a brave, but unsuccessful, stand at Thermopylae (ther-MOP-uh-LEE). The Persian navy, however, was later defeated at the Greek colony of Salamis (SAL-uh-mus) on the island of Cyprus. Xerxes then returned home and eventually abandoned his plans to take Greece.

Xerxes was the last of the great Achaemenian kings. After his assassination, in 465 B.C.E., the royal house became a place of intrigue and murder. The Achaemenian kings who followed had large harems that often included more than three hundred women. These women, some of whom had a great deal of influence with the king, bore many sons, and more than one thought that he had a claim to the throne. Because no line of succession was ever developed, a scramble for power often took place after a king died. Sometimes the king's death was hastened by one of his sons, who in turn would be murdered by a brother.

New Rulers

Persia's great wealth, and its growing weakness, made it a tempting target. In 330 B.C.E., Alexander the Great gathered a powerful army and began a drive that took him all the way to Persepolis. With its fall, the Persians once again became a conquered people. They would remain under Greek rule until 171 B.C.E.

The Greeks, who had a large empire, eventually had difficulty holding the nations they had conquered. As the Greeks grew weaker, local leaders began to assert themselves, including those of Parthia, which had once been a province of Persia. Parthian leaders declared themselves and Media free of Greek rule, then set their sights on restoring all of the old Persian Empire. By 171 B.C.E. they had begun to accomplish some of their goals, seizing land from the Greeks, a little at a time.

The Parthians continued to gain power, and they eventually became strong enough to stop an invasion by the Romans at Carrhae (KAR-ee) in 53 C.E. The Romans had replaced the Greeks as a world power. The Romans and Parthians fought many battles over the next two hundred years, struggles that seriously undermined both sides.

This Islamic miniature painting depicts an archer making a "Parthian shot." The Parthians were such excellent archers they could shoot while in retreat—real or feigned.

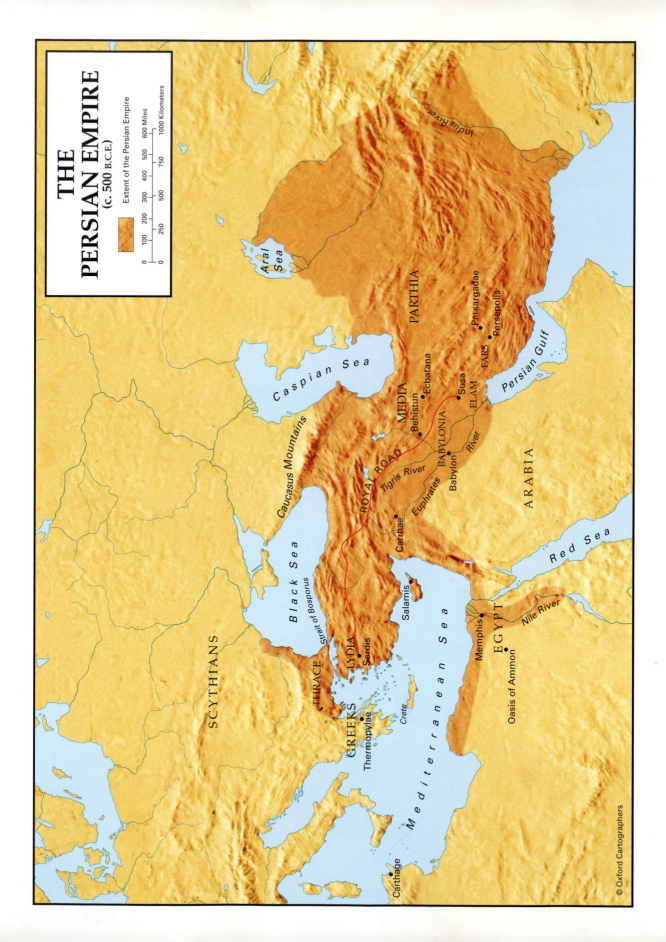

THE
PERSIAN EMPIRE
(c. 500 B.C.E.)

Extent of the Persian Empire

100	600 Miles
200	1000 Kilometers
300	500
400	750
500	250
0	0

Indus River

Aral Sea

PARTHIA

Parsargadae
Persepolis

Caspian Sea

Ecbatana
FARS

Behistun
MEDIA
Susa
ELAM

Persian Gulf

Caucasus Mountains

ROYAL ROAD

Tigris River

BABYLONIA
River

Babylon
Euphrates

ARABIA

Carrhae

Black Sea

Red Sea

Strait of Bosporus

Salamis

SCYTHIANS

Nile River

Memphis
EGYPT

THRACE
LYDIA
Sardis

Oasis of Ammon

GREEKS
Thermopylae

Crete

Mediterranean Sea

Carthage

"SUPERHORSES" AT CARRHAE

When the great Roman general Crassus met the Persians at the Battle of Carrhae, he was shocked at the sight of a new—and invincible—weapon: Parthian "super-horses." These steeds, sleek, muscular, powerful, and incredibly fast, were the result of the lifestyle changes of the Parthians and good equine bloodlines. The first Parthians were nomads, and they had little to offer their horses except the grasses on the Persian plateau. But by the time the Romans invaded Persia, the Parthians had become farmers. They now fed their horses a diet rich in grain. The result was larger and stronger horses. By breeding the best of these, the Parthians eventually developed a new breed.

Because these horses were so strong, they made perfect mounts for warfare. They could be draped in heavy protective mail, a flexible mesh made of metal, and could also carry a rider decked out in mail. Just the sight of hundreds of these gigantic steeds, charging across a battlefield bearing heavily armed soldiers, caused the bravest man to tremble with fear.

The Romans at Carrhae, with their typical short spears, quickly realized that they couldn't stop the advance of the armored men and horses, and few tried to do so. Instead the men broke ranks and ran.

Once the cavalry had forced the enemy to flee, the Parthian archers raced to the battlefield, firing volleys of arrows. The Parthian archers were so good that they could fire shots as they moved forward into battle *and* over their shoulders as they departed. The Romans had no way to defend themselves at Carrhae, and more than ten thousand were taken prisoner.

In 224 C.E. the Parthians were so weak that the Sasanians (sa-SAY-nee-anz), a tribe living in southern Persia, were able to seize control of the empire. The Sasanians claimed to be descendants of the old Achaemenian line, and they were determined to continue the Parthians' plan to restore the old empire. Gradually they added more Persian territories to their holdings. The Sasanians ruled for more than four hundred years, but like those who came before them, they gradually grew weaker and weaker.

In 642 the Sasanians were conquered by a powerful new force of invaders, the Arabs, who brought a new religion, Islam, to the region. The Arabs would control the area for hundreds of years. The ancient Persian Empire had finally come to an end.

CHAPTER TWO

A UNIQUE AND PROSPEROUS SOCIETY

Even before the Persians had a great empire, horses were important to them, especially for hunting. During the period when they were building their empire, when this sculpture was crafted, the Persians valued horses for their usefulness in the army.

Very little is known for certain about the way of life of the first Persians. They did not leave written records. In addition these people moved about often, creating only temporary settlements of which little remains. As a result archaeologists have few clues to help them determine what their lives had been like.

In fact the scant knowledge we have about these people comes from the few records of other civilizations that mentioned them. These records indicate that the ancient Persians were a hardy group who needed few luxuries. They loved to hunt wild game, racing on horseback behind their prey, which they felled with bow and arrow. And they were fiercely loyal to their tribe.

Historians have much more information about the culture of the Persians from the Achaemenian period (550–330 B.C.E.) onward. By this time, the Persians had a system of writing, which they had acquired from the Elamites and Babylonians. Also, they were establishing permanent settlements, the ruins of which historians and archaeologists have been able to study.

Although historians would like even more information about the Persians, what is available gives us a good idea of their society. It is important to remember, though, that much of what we know about the Persians comes from Greek historians, who were making their observations many years after actual events occurred. Even more important, the Greeks were enemies of the Persians. Their writings were certainly biased and need to be "taken with a grain of salt." Having understood this, we can still learn much about Persian society.

The Sasanian kings, the last rulers of ancient Persia, liked to show themselves valiantly hunting. Magnificent silver plates such as this one would have been used in the courts of these kings.

Building an Empire

Empire building had a profound effect on the way of life of the ancient Persians. It affected their army, social classes, art, diet, clothing styles, trade, and even their language. To build—and hold together—an empire, Persian kings needed many soldiers. Therefore, all males from ages fifteen to fifty were expected to

21

serve in the army when asked, and no exceptions were made. To enforce this rule, the kings made memorable examples of anyone who asked to be excused. According to one story, when a father of three sons asked King Darius to excuse one of them in order that the family might not risk losing all of them, Darius had all three killed. Military service was so highly valued that the king himself led troops into battle, and military leadership, which was considered a rare privilege, was limited to Persian nobles.

SOCIAL CLASSES

Like many ancient cultures, Persian society was divided into classes. The upper class consisted of the king, nobles, and priests. During the later days of the empire, in the Sasanian era, Persian society was complex, and nobles and their sons held positions that hadn't existed in Cyrus's time. Not all positions had the same prestige, so the upper class was divided then into four groups, called estates. The first estate consisted of royalty, priests, and judges. The second estate was limited to military leaders, while the third included scribes, physicians, astronomers, and poets. The fourth estate was made up of wealthy landholders, and it was the least prestigious.

The lower class, the vast majority of Persians, always consisted of laborers, either freemen or bondsmen. Freemen worked for wages, and they could pick and choose where they were employed. Bondsmen, who were serfs and slaves, had little choice regarding where they worked.

Serfs, and their children, who were mostly farmers, were part of the property on which they toiled. They were expected to fight for their landowner, should he lead troops into battle. If the land was transferred to another holder, the serfs, and their families, remained with the land.

Slaves, unlike serfs, could be sold whenever their owners wished to do so. However, slaves often had higher skills than serfs did. Slaves were usually prisoners of war who had been builders, bakers, or barbers in their homelands, and they were valuable assets to their owners. Their numbers increased dramatically after 500 B.C.E., as Persia conquered more and more territory.

To maintain such a large army, the ancient Persians were encouraged to marry early and raise big families. Unmarried adults were regarded as shirkers, people who were avoiding their duty, and they were looked down on. Because children were so important, abortion was considered one of the worst crimes of all, punishable by death. Men were encouraged to have more than one wife at a time, in order to produce more children. Kings had hundreds of wives.

Dwellings of Brick and Stone

The vast majority of Persian families lived in the country, where they grazed sheep or raised crops such as wheat. All the land technically belonged to the king, who then gave it to nobles and military leaders. The best leaders received the most land, which was often too large for one family to work. Therefore, Persians who did not have land of their own lived on a noble's estate and worked for him in exchange for a portion of the crop.

Persian homes varied according to a family's wealth. Workers' homes were simple. Wood was scarce, but clay dirt was not, so walls were constructed of sun-dried bricks made from a mixture of mud and straw. Roofs were made of mud, straw, and rushes on a timber frame. A fireplace provided warmth in winter, and thick walls kept out the heat in summer. Since wood furniture was expensive, most Persians couldn't afford many pieces. Instead, they sat and slept on the rugs that covered the floors. Dishes and cooking pots were made of clay.

The homes of nobles were more luxurious. Usually they were made of blocks of limestone or bricks baked in ovens. Thick carpets covered the floors. Furniture included numerous chairs, beds, and tables, which were often set with silver plates and golden goblets.

The most elegant homes were built around a courtyard containing shade trees, pools, and beautiful flowers. Wealthy Persians often created shady gardens where they could escape from their uncomfortably hot and dry climate. Each garden was surrounded by a wall to keep out the wind. Inside the walls, owners dug a pond in the middle of a long narrow plot of land. This pond was fed by a *qanat*, part of a large, sophisticated irrigation system that brought water from mountain streams many miles away.

Persian gardens overflowed with lush vegetation. Large trees—cypresses, elms, and maples—provided shade. Fruit trees added fragrance and beauty when they blossomed, as well as

IF YOU LIVED IN ANCIENT PERSIA

If you had been born during the reign of the Achaemenian kings in Persia, your way of life would have been determined by the facts of your birth—whether you were a girl or a boy, noble or commoner, or a relative of the king. With this chart you can trace the course your life might have taken if you grew up as a noble in one of Persia's most magnificent capitals.

You were born in Persepolis. . . .

As a Boy . . .   As a Girl . . .

You live in a simple one-story house with a garden courtyard. Here you are cared for during your first five years, the most vulnerable time of your life, by your mother, other female relatives, and servants. You don't see your father very often, so that he doesn't become too attached to you and suffer if you should die.

At age 5 you are placed under the care of your father. He makes sure that you learn how to be a good warrior, to ride a horse well, to shoot with a bow and arrow, and above all, to tell the truth at all times. You may learn how to read and write.

At age 5 you remain at home and begin to learn homemaking skills. You probably do not learn to read and write. You learn how to spin thread and weave cloth, how to sing and play an instrument.

At age 13 or 14 your parents choose a very young girl to be a wife for you, although the wedding will not take place for a few years. It is considered lucky to marry a close relative, even a half sister or an aunt. You will probably have several wives by the time you are 25.

At age 11 or 12 your parents choose a husband for you, a boy a few years older. Your parents give his family a large dowry, a gift of precious metals, land, and servants that will remain yours after you are married.

At age 15 you become an adult. During the ceremony marking your passage into adulthood, you put on a "sacred girdle," or belt, and you are said to be "invested with eloquence."

At age 15 you become an adult and marry. The ideal bride is supposed to be "faultless, untouched, wearing earrings." You move into the home of your husband's family.

At age 18 you enter the military. When you return from battle, you are expected to marry several women, have many children, and serve the king in his royal court and army.

As a wife and mother you take care of your home, have many children, and spend your days quietly in the harem with the other wives. You may not see any man other than your husband, even your father. You are permitted to own considerable property, and conduct all of your business from the home.

Persian tradition places great value on home and family. When you are elderly you are respected and well cared for. When you die you are not buried, for your body must not come into contact with soil. Your body is exposed to scavengers, and your bleached bones are carefully stored in stone containers.

fresh fruit in late summer and fall. Ancient varieties of orange, pear, cherry, peach, and pomegranate trees thrived. Flowering shrubs, especially climbing roses, were grown for their rich fragrance, and flowers were planted just for color.

Some of the most famous gardeners in Persia included the Achaemenian kings. Cyrus was very proud of his garden at Sardis. He planted many of the trees and shrubs himself, and according to Greek visitors it was "stocked with everything good and valuable that the soil will produce."

Surrounded by Works of Art

Persian nobles wanted delicate vases, beautiful sculptures, and luxurious fabrics with which to decorate their homes. They reached out to all parts of their vast empire for many kinds of luxury goods. The products were transported into Persia on a network of military roads built to unite the empire, the longest of which ran from Susa to Sardis, more than 1,600 miles (2,574 kilometers).

Only the homes of the richest Persians would have had pieces as elaborate as this drinking vessel in the shape of a goat. This type of cup is called a rhyton. It has two openings, the large one at the top and a smaller one between the animal's front legs. The drinker would hold the cup in the air, and as someone poured wine into the top, the drinker would catch it in his mouth as it poured out of the smaller hole.

The palaces of kings, like the homes of nobles, were awe-inspiring buildings designed to command respect. The palaces were an unusual blend of materials gathered from countries all over the empire. Darius's palace at Susa, for instance, contained timber from Lebanon, gold from Sardis, silver and ebony from Egypt, and ivory from Ethiopia. In addition the palace was a mix of styles and techniques, for it was built by stonecutters from Ionia, goldsmiths from Media and Egypt, woodworkers from Sardis, and glazed-brick makers from Babylonia. The result, though, was uniquely Persian.

Artisans from all over the empire also created most of the stone monuments and carvings in capital cities such as Persepolis and Behistun (BAY-his-TOON), where a large monument to King Darius is located. Lacking granite or marble, the Persians used

Unlike Persepolis, the Persian capital of Susa was not close to any sources of stone. Instead it was decorated with hundreds of figures made of bricks. These bricks were created in molds and then painted with colorful glazes before they were fired in a kiln, or oven.

what they had on hand, blocks and cliffs of limestone.

Stone carvings often reflected Persia's pride in its military conquests, and victorious leaders and defeated foes were the carvings' main themes. Women, who couldn't play any part in the army, usually weren't portrayed, unless they were goddesses. Therefore, we have few "pictures" of ordinary or even royal women from this historical period.

Toward the end of the Achaemenian period, Persians began to make greater use of the wealth of materials coming into the

country to create works of art. They also turned local supplies of silver into fine jewelry and Persian wool into plush carpets. These carpets were valued highly for their intricate designs, usually illustrations of flower gardens or hunting parties, and their thick pile, the short, thin strands of wool that are tied to the carpet's backing and stand on end. Many carpets had a pile containing more than two hundred strands of wool to the square inch. Persian carpets were indeed works of art, and there were many eager buyers throughout the empire.

DARIUS, ROYAL BUILDER

Darius personally chose the location for Persepolis, one of several capitals, for sentimental and practical reasons. First of all, the site, a rocky plateau that rose high above its surroundings, was located in the center of Fars, the first area to be settled by Darius's ancestors and therefore considered sacred. Second, any settlement located on the plateau would be easy to defend. Enemies could be spotted far away as they crossed the surrounding flatlands, and invaders also made easy targets when they tried to climb the cliff of the plateau.

By 520 B.C.E. Darius's plans were complete, and he assembled the best construction workers from all over his empire. Workers built a retaining wall around the edge of the plateau to fortify it. They shaped the plateau's surface so that the capital would have three levels, making it possible for visitors to see many buildings at one glance. Finally they created an elaborate water-pumping system, chiseling waterways through solid rock.

When the groundwork was completed, more workers and artisans were brought in. Some made two broad stairways, from huge squares of limestone, that led to the top of the plateau. These stairs, which sculptors decorated with elaborate carvings, were wide enough to accommodate ten mounted soldiers, riding side by side. Other artisans built an impressive entrance to the capital, gold-plated doors that were flanked by giant statues of winged bulls.

Most workers, however, were assigned to the *apadana,* an audience hall. When finished, the hall was big enough to hold ten thousand people. The roof was held in place by pillars sixty feet tall, elaborately decorated with gold and jewels. The *apadana*'s walls were covered with pictures, created from brightly colored tiles, of animals and flowers.

The audience hall was just one of many beautiful buildings. When the capital was finished, it had three palaces, one each for Darius, Xerxes, and Artaxerxes, complete with gold thrones. Persepolis also had a council hall. It was approached by a stairway, which was decorated with figures of men carved from stone, two per step. Each figure represented one of the satrapies, or provinces, in the Persian Empire, and the men were pictured bearing gifts to the king. Door jambs were made of black stone, which was polished until it shone like ebony, and statues of lions, bulls, and monsters stood everywhere. It's no wonder that historians have called this capital one of the finest in the ancient world.

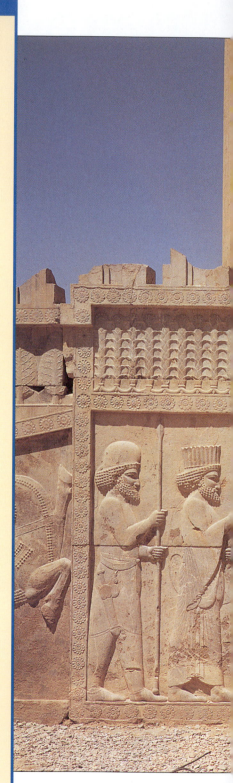

The remains of the apadana, *the once-spectacular audience hall that Darius built at Persepolis*

The magnificent sculptures on the cliffs at Behistun show the triumph of Darius over the rulers of lands who rebelled against him. The victorious king is portrayed stepping on the neck of a foe. The long inscription below the scene lists the provinces of his empire that "brought tribute to me . . . in the night time as in the day time." He proudly declares, "I am king of kings." Rising more than 1,700 feet (518 meters) above the plain, the sculpture and inscription could be seen for miles around.

Food and Clothing

Traditionally, Persians ate only one meal a day, not from necessity as much as from custom. They believed that too much food would make them fat and weak. But as tasty produce began to arrive from all parts of the empire, Persians couldn't resist the temptation to consume more food, and their eating habits changed dramatically. They had always had an abundant supply of wheat, meat, and wine at home, and now they added honey, citrus fruits, dates, dried fish, and spices from India to their daily diets. Eventually lengthy banquets became fashionable; guests still ate one meal, only it lasted all day long!

Persian clothing was also influenced by people in their empire. Some Persians copied the Median style, then modified it to fit their own needs. Persians considered it indecent to show any part of their bodies except their faces, so they swathed themselves in garments from head to toe. Women's clothing styles probably differed little from men's. Men wore long robes gathered at the waist with lots of folds. They wore sandals or leather shoes, and they topped their hair, arranged in tight ringlets, with a cap or turban. Men also sported long beards. They wore wool in the winter; white linen, an extremely durable fabric, was a favorite for summer clothing among the nobility because it was cool and lightweight. Wealthy Persians could afford to splurge on luxurious fabrics, and they often wore imported silk.

Well-to-do Persians also loved to decorate themselves with lots and lots of gold jewelry and precious stones. Both men and women wore rings, earrings, and bracelets set with imported pearls, rubies, emeralds, and lapis lazuli, a brilliant blue stone.

The variety of goods available only whetted the Persians' appetite for more. King Darius sent men on expeditions to discover new resources. He also improved existing ports and built a canal connecting the Nile River to the Red Sea to make trade easier between the Arabian and the Mediterranean seas.

In the Achaemenid period, wealthy Persians favored stiff necklaces, called torques, and bracelets, which ended in the heads of animals, such as lions and rams. This type of gold jewelry was expertly made, crafted with tiny pieces of colorful, precious stones.

Trade, Money, and Record Keeping

International trading created the need for money. The Lydians were the first to use coins to replace the barter system—trading one item for another—and the Persians decided to imitate them and create a coin that would be recognized and accepted throughout the empire. The new system made buying and selling much easier. Sellers anywhere were willing to take something they knew had value—a coin—in exchange for their product, rather than take a questionable product from a stranger.

As trade grew, so did the need for keeping records. The Achaemenians hired scribes from Babylonia, who recorded

This gold plaque from the reign of Darius I has the same inscription written in cuneiform in three different languages: Persian, Babylonian, and the ancient Iranian language Elamite. The Babylonians from Mesopotamia were the first to use cuneiform, beginning around 3300 B.C.E. Their Elamite neighbors used this script to write their own language, and under Darius it was used for Persian as well.

accounts in their language, Akkadian, which became the official language of the Persian Empire. Old Persian was also put into writing during King Darius's reign. Darius's scribes adopted a system of writing from their neighbors the Elamites and the Babylonians. Known as cuneiform, the script used wedge-shaped symbols to represent sounds.

Although the Persians finally had a written language, the majority of them remained illiterate. This does not mean that they didn't have stories or poetry. They had both, but tales and poems were always presented from memory.

Storytelling was only one form of entertainment. The Persians were also fond of music, and they played harps, flutes, and tambourines, and sang songs.

A Different Way to Govern

The Persian kings developed a unique system to govern their empire. Eventually all the conquered nations were divided into twenty provinces, or satrapies (SA-trah-peez). The kings controlled these conquered areas by putting them under the authority of trusted Persian soldiers and generals. To make sure the generals were doing what they were supposed to do, the kings sent inspectors to the satrapies regularly. The kings also appointed secretaries in the provinces to keep an eye on the generals and the inspectors.

To encourage peace and loyalty in the defeated nations, their citizens were allowed to practice their ancient customs and follow their religious beliefs. This was an unusual approach for the time, since most rulers tried to force their ways on the people they conquered. This tolerance lessened the hostility toward the new rulers, but it did not erase all desire to be free of the Persians.

There were advantages to being part of the Persian Empire. Because the enormous Persian army needed large quantities of food, satrapies were encouraged to raise more crops to feed the troops as well as the citizens. At its height the empire numbered forty million people. To help produce this foodstuff, the Persians introduced rice to Mesopotamia and alfalfa to Greece, where both crops flourished. The ancient Persians also experimented with livestock and may have been the first to domesticate chickens, a practice they spread throughout the empire. In addition, although the Persians willingly went to war to expand their empire, there were long periods of peace and prosperity, which all citizens in the empire enjoyed.

New Influences, New Heights

When the Greeks conquered Persia, they tried to modify Persian culture by blending it with Greek culture, taking the best of both societies. To help this process along, Alexander the Great started Greek colonies and cities in the Persian Empire. The results of such an ambitious program were mixed. Some Persians readily accepted the new cities and all they had to offer: Greek art, literature, and lifestyle. A few Persian artisans even went as far as to imitate Greek art, topping columns in Persian temples with Grecian capitals and carving goddesses in long, flowing Grecian gowns. The majority of Persians, though, especially those living in the country, ignored Greek cities, settlers, and ideas.

Once the Parthians had driven out the Greeks, they tried to reduce the Greek influence and bring back the grandeur of the Achaemenians. The Parthians redesigned the Greek cities, which were laid out in straight lines. The circular settlements they created may have resembled their old military camps. They sculpted their military history, Achaemenian style, into limestone cliffs. But because they lacked the wealth and the huge empire the Achaemenians had had, the Parthians were forced to work with local materials and craftsmen. The result was a culture that was truly Persian.

For example, the Parthians experimented with architectural forms, and they invented the *iwan* (EE-won). *Iwans* were three-sided brick hallways with high curved ceilings shaped like half-barrels. The open end faced a shaded courtyard. Not only did the high ceiling permit a view of the sky as one walked toward the yard, but the *iwan* allowed air to move freely throughout the house, cooling it during the hot Persian summers.

These unusual ceilings were made possible by creating a new use for paget stone, which is found in many parts of Persia. The Parthians discovered that when powder from this stone was mixed with water, it formed a quick-drying, durable mortar. To make an *iwan*, the Parthians built the ceiling brick by brick, spreading a little mortar, then holding the brick in place until the mortar dried.

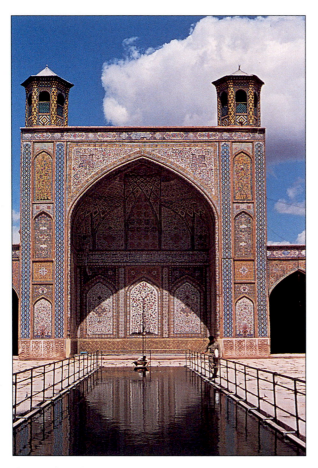

Long after the ancient Persians had fallen, the iwan *continued to be important in the architecture of the region.*

The Parthians also made use of local supplies of silver. Artisans turned the precious metal into beautiful silver plates and bowls, which were decorated with brave warriors or hunters on horseback closing in on their prey. These became very popular in Persia as well as in Europe and China.

When the Sasanians came to power, they continued to build on the Parthians' work. Metalwork flourished. And while silver plates continued to portray warriors and hunters, two new artistic themes—inspired by the Greeks and Romans—appeared: beautiful women and royal banquets. At this time also, elaborate silver crowns for royalty became the style. Some were so heavy the kings could not wear them. Instead the crowns were hung above the kings' thrones. Numerous bronze statues were also made. And in the oldest of traditions, artisans continued to make Persian rugs and carve monuments on cliffs, portraying their greatest military achievements.

When the Arabs conquered the Persian Empire, they, like the Greeks, tried to change the culture. They were not as successful as they had hoped to be, and many ancient Persian customs and crafts continued to be practiced for hundreds of years.

Right: *The Sasanians are known for their magnificent skills in creating elegant objects of silver and gold. This life-size sculpture shows the king wearing an elaborate crown with a crescent moon at its front. It is not known which of the Sasanian kings is portrayed here.*

CHAPTER THREE

WORSHIPING THE GODS

Like most ancient people, the first Persians believed in many gods and demons. They also believed that their gods were fickle; they might be kind one day and cruel the next, depending on how they felt.

To make the gods happy and gain favors, the Persians worshiped their deities often. They prayed three times a day, and on special occasions they made sacrifices of prized bulls, which were slaughtered during a religious ceremony and roasted over a roaring fire. It was believed that the deities would be attracted by the aroma of the meat while it cooked. As they hovered above the flames, the gods would be strengthened by the fragrances rising from the fire. Thus fortified, the gods would be able to fight evil spirits and perform other tasks, such as bringing rain or assuring victory in a coming battle.

Although this bronze sculpture from Susa is even more ancient than the Persians, it shows the type of sacrificial rituals that the Persians may have practiced.

Ancient Deities

The first Persians worshiped many gods and goddesses. Among the most important were Anahita, the earth goddess; Mithra, the sun god; Tishtrya (tish-TREE-a), the storm god; and Haoma (ho-MA), a god of eternal life. The Persians had little access to fertile land and little available water to irrigate their crops and sustain life. Therefore it is easy to understand why they valued their limited resources and regarded land and water as sacred. Anahita was the source of all fertility. She provided rich soil and all the water on earth as well as

human offspring. If she was strong and willing to bless them, the ancient Persians could have many children and, with the help of the sun god, produce abundant crops.

Tishtrya, the storm god, took many shapes. He was sometimes thought of as a powerful white horse that would race into the ocean, creating huge waves that reached the sky. The waves were caught up and held in the clouds until they reached Persia, where they dropped their moisture as the annual spring rains.

While Anahita, Mithra, and Tishtrya sustained life on earth,

This monstrous-looking creature is really a protective spirit. It takes the form of a lion with the horns of a ram and the wings and hind feet of a bird of prey. This good demon's job was to scare off evil spirits.

This Persian painting from the fourteenth century shows the simurgh, *or heavenly dragon, on the slopes of Mount Alburz.*

Haoma made immortality possible. According to ancient beliefs, Haoma died and rose again. He then gave humankind some of his blood to drink. This blood brought eternal life to all who drank it. Haoma takes the form of a bull in Persian mythology.

These ancient deities—along with giants, fairies, and the *simurgh* (see-MURG), a mythical dragonlike creature with a peacock's tail—lived on Mount Alburz. It was the highest mountain in the world, located in the center of the earth. The sun, moon, and stars circled this mountain, which was a massive emerald. And it was at Mount Alburz that the Chinvat bridge began, stretching from its summit to heaven, making it possible for the souls of good men and women to reach paradise.

CHINVAT BRIDGE

The Chinvat bridge was the place where good and bad souls were separated as they tried to reach paradise. If the dead person had been good, the bridge was wide, and a beautiful young woman assisted the soul on its journey. If the deceased had been evil, the bridge eventually narrowed to the width of a knife blade, and an ugly old hag jumped out of the shadows to frighten the soul so that it would fall into hell.

Whenever the gods left Mount Alburz, humankind was affected. When Tishtrya, the storm god, left, he brought rain—only, however, if he was strong enough to defeat the drought demon. He had to be sufficiently strengthened by worship and sacrifices to do so.

Zoroaster's God of Gods

Religious beliefs in Persia changed radically when Zoroaster (ZOR-uh-as-ter) began to preach. Historians are not certain when the founder of the new religion was born, but most believe that he lived around 1000 B.C.E. He stunned the ancient Persians by announcing that there was a supreme god, Ahura-Mazda (a-HOO-ra-MAZ-da). This god, Zoroaster said, had created everything that was good—heaven, earth, men, women, joy, light, fire, and a guardian angel for every person on earth.

Ahura-Mazda had seven holy spirits to assist him. These

ZOROASTER

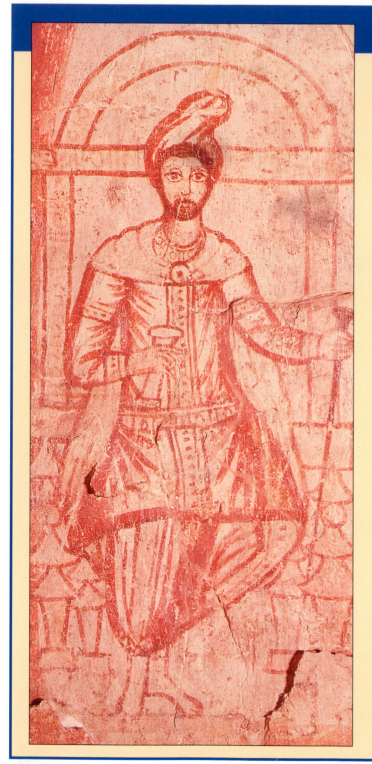

Little is known for certain about the life of Zoroaster. He was a member of the priesthood known as the magi. He probably began to study for his profession when he was seven years old. After becoming a priest at fifteen, he often wandered in the wilderness. There, in isolation, he sought a solution to the problems that bothered him the most: warfare and injustice.

When Zoroaster was thirty years old, it is said that he was approached by a ghostly figure surrounded by brilliant light. The figure led him into the presence of Ahura-Mazda. Here he received instructions about how humankind should live so that there would be peace and justice for all. Ahura-Mazda gave Zoroaster the Book of Knowledge and ordered him to spread its contents throughout the world.

Zoroaster devoted the rest of his life to preaching the truths he found in this book. When he was very old, a huge bolt of lightning struck the earth. As the lightning returned to the sky, it took Zoroaster upward with it, lifting him to heaven.

A portrait of Zoroaster from Syria. The Parthian army spread the worship of Zoroaster to many parts of the ancient world.

spirits represented abstract ideas: the Good Mind, Righteousness, Divine Will, Humility, Perfection, Immortality, and Obedience. In addition to helping people achieve specific goals—humility or righteousness, for example—each spirit was responsible for protecting something good on earth, such as fire or truth.

Like Persian society, Zoroastrianism divided its gods into classes. Ahura-Mazda was supreme, and he ruled in paradise. His seven holy spirits, the second class, assisted in heaven and on earth. The third class, old Persian deities, such as Anahita, performed their deeds on earth. Whether or not Zoroaster encouraged the worship of the old gods is not clear. He did, however, discourage animal sacrifice. Zoroaster believed that animals were too valuable to kill, especially bulls; farmers needed them to work the fields.

The Evil One

Ahura-Mazda was opposed by Ahriman, his twin brother, who was known as the Evil One. Ahriman created everything that was bad—serpents, vermin, locusts, winter, darkness, and sin. He ruined paradise, where the first humans lived, by bringing evil into the world. Ahriman was also served by seven spirits, each one of whom was out to tempt humankind to sin.

The idea of one supreme god was novel, even shocking, to the Persians. Zoroaster also told his followers that they could *choose* between being good or evil; their lives were not controlled by the gods, as previously believed. If they chose a righteous life, they would be rewarded for their efforts; when they died, their souls would join Ahura-Mazda in heaven. If they chose to do evil acts, however, they would join Ahriman in hell.

One of Zoroaster's followers, Viraf, had a vision in which he visited both heaven and hell. He described for the Persians what he had seen: Heaven, again like ancient Persian society, was divided into social classes. Good kings, for example, had a place all their own, as did farmers and artisans. Dutiful wives who treated their husbands well also had a specific place in paradise, where light, happiness, flowers, and trees were abundant.

Hell, on the other hand, was a miserable place. Here, bad men and women suffered more during their first three nights than they had throughout their whole lives on earth. They were

Ahura-Mazda, the supreme god of the Zoroastrians, was often represented as a winged sun such as the one appearing over these sphinxes. This scene, made of glazed bricks, comes from an ancient Persian palace at the royal city of Susa.

exposed to extreme temperatures, constant darkness, and a putrid smell. As if that wasn't enough, each person was punished according to his or her crimes. A man who had cheated people by giving false measurements in business deals was forever after made to measure dust and ashes, which he was then forced to eat. A ruler who had been unmerciful was beaten by fifty demons. A selfish man was stretched taut on a rack and punished by a thousand demons who jumped on him with great vigor.

Ahura-Mazda at first tried to stop Ahriman. When he failed to do so, Ahura-Mazda offered to set a time limit—a period of twelve thousand years—during which the two gods would struggle for human souls. At the end of this period Ahura-Mazda would judge all humankind and reunite the bodies and souls of the righteous. Ahriman accepted this limit, and the battle for souls began.

The monumental struggle between good and evil made each person's actions very important. When anyone chose to do a bad thing, it was regarded as an act of worship that strengthened the Evil One. This enabled Ahriman to bring more wickedness—and more misery—into the world. It also explained why bad things happened. When Persians chose to perform good deeds, they strengthened Ahura-Mazda, making a victory over evil and misery possible.

The Book of Knowledge

To help people lead a righteous life, Zoroaster was given instructions by Ahura-Mazda which were recorded in the Zend-Avesta (zen-dah-VES-tah), or Book of Knowledge. This became the Zoroastrians' holy book. Actually the work of many authors, some of whom lived long before Zoroaster, the Zend-Avesta was composed of three parts: a religious history of the Persians (the Vendida); a collection of litanies, formal prayers and responses used during religious ceremonies (the Visparad); and ancient hymns, some of which are believed to have been composed by Zoroaster (the Yasna).

Even though Zoroaster at first was ridiculed for his new beliefs, Vishtaspa, a powerful prince in what is now northeastern Iran, accepted the prophet's ideas. Other nobles followed, and eventually even the Achaemenian kings accepted Zoroastrianism.

In the Zoroastrian story of the first man and the first woman on earth, it is the evil Ahriman who tempts the first couple with an apple.

After the kings became believers, Zoroastrianism flourished in Persia, reaching its height during King Darius's rule, when it became the state religion.

While the ancient Persians had allowed their subject peoples the freedom to worship their own gods, the conquerors of Persia were not as tolerant. The Greeks opposed Zoroastrianism; they wanted the Persians to be more like them and worship Greek gods. When they defeated Persia, the Greeks tried to eliminate Zoroastrianism by killing many magi, or priests. Since most beliefs and instructions for proper behavior were handed down orally through the priests, their deaths were a devastating loss to the faith.

Once Zoroastrianism was weakened, many Persians, disheartened by the Greek conquest from which their god did not protect them, replaced Ahura-Mazda with other deities. Some Persians adopted Greek gods; others elevated old Persian gods to take the place of Ahura-Mazda, often giving them more responsibilities. Mithra, for example, became the god of war as well as the sun god.

When the Parthians drove out the Greeks almost two hundred years later, Parthian kings attempted to restore Zoroastrianism as the main religion. King Vologesus (vo-luh-GAY-seez) V gave orders that all old scriptures—once believed to have been so extensive that they covered twelve thousand cowhides—should be found and preserved. However, only a small portion of the scriptures was ever recovered.

Vologesus then ordered all believers who had memorized lessons to come forward to recite the passages to scribes. Even this move failed to re-create many of Zoroaster's teachings, and the Parthian dream of restoring Zoroastrianism to its former position failed.

The magus, or priest, of ancient Persia on this gold plaque is identified by the bundle of twigs he carries, a symbol of the priesthood.

THE MAGI

The magi, or priests, were members of the highest class of society in Persia. They inherited their positions. Until the time of Zoroaster, they did not support any particular religion. Instead they simply assisted Persians in worshiping the god of their choice, conducting sacrifices, and studying the stars to forecast the future. When Zoroastrianism became the state religion of Persia, the magi became its spokesmen and defenders.

Perhaps the best-known magi were Gasper, Melchior, and Balthazar. According to legend, the three used a brilliant star to find Christ's birthplace, where they presented him with gold, frankincense, and myrrh. For centuries, Western artists have depicted this scene, known as the Adoration of the Magi. The magi have also been immortalized in a Christmas carol, "We Three Kings of Orient Are."

At the same time, those who had remained faithful to Zoroastrianism argued among themselves. Since so many of Zoroaster's lessons had been destroyed or handed down orally—which is not as accurate as writing down the lessons—no one knew for certain what Zoroaster had said. Different leaders claimed that they knew the truth, however, and several distinct groups developed within the religion, further weakening it.

A group known as the Zurvanites became the most influential. Zurvanites believed that Ahura-Mazda and Ahriman were sons of Zurvan, whose name means "time." Zurvan was a force that had always existed, and until the creation of his sons, a force that was all alone. Once his two sons were born, they battled for supremacy on earth. Although humanity would be affected by the struggle between good and evil, men and women had no part to play in the drama. Therefore there was no reward or punishment, no heaven or hell.

Bold Challengers

Zoroastrianism was further weakened by the founding of two new religions. One was started in the third century C.E. by Mani, who took portions of several religions—Zoroastrianism, Christianity, Buddhism—and created a new faith, Manichaeism (MAN-uh-key-iz-uhm). The second new religion was started in the fifth century by a man named Mazdak.

Mazdakism was as much a social revolution as a new religious idea. Mazdak believed that the inequalities among the social classes caused hatred; they were the source of evil thoughts and deeds. Therefore social classes were to be abolished. To end economic differences, Mazdak told the rich that they should share their wealth with the poor. To end royal bloodlines, he told the nobles that they should give their wives to the peasants, an idea that enraged the nobles. Mazdak's beliefs appealed to the serfs, though, and the threat of social upheaval was so great that he was arrested and put to death.

The Persian people turned to these new religions in part because of the many problems in the empire during both the Parthian and Sasanian eras: droughts, weakened military forces, and threats of invasion by the Romans. The Persians hoped, just as

MANI

Mani was born on April 14, 216 C.E., in Babylonia, where he spent most of his childhood. Like his father, a member of a noble Parthian family, Mani showed a strong interest in religion.

Mani studied everything he could about various religions before making his first public appearance as a prophet in 242. After selecting what he regarded as the best ideas from different faiths, he announced that there was only one god. This god, over the years, had sent a divine messenger to earth to show people the way to salvation. The messenger had appeared as various men—Noah, Buddha, and Jesus, for example, as well as other religious leaders, including Mani.

The path to heaven for Mani's followers was anything but easy. Because he believed that all worldly things were evil, he expected his followers to reject everything but the basics: a little food, clothing, and simple shelter. The more earthly things Manicheans could avoid, the more likely it was that they could enter heaven.

Mani traveled in Persia and the surrounding areas with twelve disciples, preaching to enthusiastic crowds. Eventually Manicheans could be found throughout Persia and as far as China and North Africa.

The magi became alarmed by Mani's popularity, and they begged the king of Persia to have him arrested. At first the king refused to do so, protecting Mani's right to worship as he pleased. But when Mani accused the magi of performing evil acts, the king ordered his arrest.

Sources differ as to what happened next. Most historians believe that Mani spent the rest of his life in jail. But according to legend, Mani was crucified, and his corpse was defiled. Large pieces of his skin supposedly were stripped from his body and hung in public places as a warning to others who might want to oppose the powerful magi.

they had after the Greek conquest, that these problems could be solved with divine help. New interpretations of old beliefs, and different gods, they felt, would provide the assistance they needed. The question of which religion to choose, however, was decided for them in 642, when the Arabs took control and forced the ancient Persians to worship their god, Allah.

CHAPTER FOUR

PUTTING FAITH INTO ACTION

This small statue wears the crown and garments of an Achaemenid king. The bottom of the figure's feet are pierced, and the statue may have originally been attached to a piece of furniture in a palace or temple.

The fierce Persians of the battlefield were exceptionally gentle in their homeland. Following deeply held religious beliefs, they tried hard to perform good deeds that would strengthen and please their god Ahura-Mazda. Their devotion greatly affected their culture, and their religious beliefs were the basis of many of their laws.

The ancient Persians, however, made no effort to spread their faith and its customs throughout the empire. They believed that their religion was meant for them only, a gift from their god who had selected them as his own special people. In addition, they sometimes regarded the people they conquered as supporters of the Evil One, unworthy of life everlasting.

Stamping Out the Evil Lie

Persians, like all religious people, had a list of forbidden activities. Of all the sins people might commit, few, the Persians believed, were worse than lying. This emphasis on honesty was, in part, a result of their earliest way of life. The first nomadic Persians had to cooperate with each other, and with their neighboring tribes, in order to survive. A barterer who lied about the value of a horse being traded could cause a serious conflict among tribal members. Likewise, nomadic tribes had to make and honor agreements among themselves as to which people would graze horses and sheep on a particular piece of land, if all the tribes were to have a fair share.

Once Zoroastrianism became popular and followers believed that every lie strengthened the Evil One, truthfulness became even more important. It was their well-known hatred of lying that gave the Persians their reputation for honesty. When they made an agreement, even with their most hated enemies,

Although the Persians did not try to convert others to their religious beliefs, their art was sometimes influenced by other cultures. This extraordinary drinking vessel, from the end of the Sasanian period, shows a strong Indian influence.

everyone knew that they would keep their word.

Most Persians had no written contracts to which they could refer when someone was accused of lying. Instead, the accused were put to a test to determine whether they were telling the truth. One test was the ordeal by water. When given a signal, the accused would pray to the god of truth, then submerge himself in water. He would remain under water while an arrow was shot and then retrieved by the fastest runner in the community. If he was still alive when the arrow was returned, he was considered innocent, for surely the god of truth, who would never protect a liar, had saved his life.

A second test was the ordeal by fire. The accused was ordered to run through a narrow opening between two roaring fires. After praying to Mithra, who destroyed liars, the accused rushed through the passageway. If he lived, he was considered innocent.

Honoring Gifts from the Gods

Water and fire had long been considered special by the Persians, not only because they exposed liars but also because they had been created by Ahura-Mazda. This made them sacred, and they were honored often with small sacrifices.

To show respect for water, the ancient Persians occasionally placed three offerings, a small amount of milk and two leaves, in a stream or river. The milk and the leaves represented the animal and plant kingdoms, neither of which could exist without water. In addition to showing respect, the offerings were meant to "feed," or strengthen the water. Because this was a good deed, it also bolstered Ahura-Mazda in his struggle against evil.

Since water was sacred, the Persians were careful to protect it from pollution. No one was allowed to put a dead or unclean item into a stream. Bathing or washing clothes in a river was forbidden. When water was needed for cleaning—which was often, for the ancient Persians valued cleanliness—it was drawn off from its source and taken to homes.

In addition to making small sacrifices to water, Persians made three offerings to the family's fire: clean wood, incense or sprigs of fragrant dried herbs, and a small piece of animal fat.

These offerings were made three times a day (the number three was considered sacred by the Persians) at mealtimes, when prayers for their country were said. (Persians did not pray for themselves, for that was considered selfish.) The wood, herbs, and fat, like the milk and leaves, were meant to strengthen the fire, and the small amount of fat produced a reassuring flare-up.

Because Persians made sacrifices to fire, they were thought to be fire worshipers. This may have been true during their early history, when a blazing fire kept them from freezing. By 600 B.C.E., however, most Persians considered fire to be of sacred origin. They believed it was created by Ahura-Mazda and brought to earth by the fire god Atar in a bolt of lightning that set some wood ablaze.

Modern Zoroastrians living in India are sometimes called Parsees, a word that comes from Persia. These modern Zoroastrians still tend the sacred fires. At a Parsee fire ceremony, people look on while the masked priest performs the ritual.

Eventually Zoroastrians added to fire's importance by regarding it as a sacred symbol of Ahura-Mazda himself, the most powerful light in the universe.

At first, fires were simply built on the ground or in hearths in homes, but by the time King Darius began his rule and Zoroastrianism was strong, fire altars started to appear in Persia. These altars, which may have been suggested to the Persians by altars they saw in conquered countries, were raised platforms designed to hold large blazes. The king had the largest and highest altar, to reflect his position in society.

Over the years fire rituals changed among the magi. Instead of tending fires on altars, some priests began to care for the sacred symbol in fire temples, tall, windowless stone buildings that were unique to the area. Using fire temples was a major change for the Persians. They didn't even have temples for their gods because they didn't believe that a deity should be confined to a building when it could be free to enjoy the beauty of nature. The change in attitude may have been the result of the influence of the Greeks, who built temples to their gods in Persia.

The fires housed in the Persian temples received the utmost care from the magi. Eventually, these fires came to be regarded as so sacred that they could not be seen by unbelievers or even touched by pure sunlight. To avoid polluting the flames, the priests burned only fragrant sandalwood and wore masks to avoid contaminating the flame with foul breath or spittle.

Making Sacrifices to the Gods

Fire was also used during sacrificial ceremonies, which had to be conducted in a specific manner by the magi. First, the land on which the sacrifice was to take place was protected from demons by being sprinkled with water. Then a fire was built and prayers were said. The name of the god being honored was called out just before the animal to be sacrificed, usually a bull, was killed by the priest. The animal was then cut up, cooked, placed on a bed of greens, and offered to the worshipers who had gathered to watch the service.

According to the legend of the god Haoma, his blood—given

HERODOTUS REPORTS ON THE PERSIANS

Herodotus, a famous Greek historian born about 480 B.C.E., traveled throughout the ancient world to study other cultures. Because the Persians had been a powerful enemy of the Greeks, he was especially interested in them. Herodotus spent many years among the Persians, recording their battles, their religious beliefs, and their way of life. He found many of their religious practices strange, as this firsthand report shows:

The following are certain Persian customs [that] I can describe from personal knowledge. The erection of statues, temples, and altars is not an accepted practice amongst them, and anyone who does such a thing is considered a fool. . . . They sacrifice to [Ahura-Mazda] from the tops of mountains. They also worship the sun, moon, and earth, fire, water, and winds, which are their only original deities. . . .

They consider telling lies more disgraceful than anything else, and, next to that, owing money. There are many reasons for their horror of debt, but the chief is their conviction that a man who owes money is bound also to tell lies. . . .

They have a profound reverence for rivers. They will never pollute a river with urine or spittle, or even wash their hands in one or allow anyone else to do so.

All this I am able to state definitely from personal knowledge. There is another practice . . . concerning the burial of the dead, which is not spoken of openly and is something of a mystery: a male Persian is never buried until the body has been torn by a bird or a dog. I know for certain that the magi have this custom, for they are quite open about it.

The magi are a peculiar caste, quite different from Egyptian priests and indeed from any other sort of person. The Egyptian priests make it an article of religion to kill no living creature except for sacrifice, but the magi not only kill anything, except dogs and men, with their own hands, [they] make a special point of doing so; ants, snakes, animals, birds—no matter what, they kill them indiscriminately. Well, it is an ancient custom, so let them keep it.

to the first Persians after his death—granted them immortality. Instead of blood, later worshipers drank a liquid that contained a mind-altering drug, called *haoma*, in his honor. This drug was obtained from an herb that grew in the mountains, and it made users feel very powerful. When taken in large amounts, it produced a drunken state that, like sacrifices, appalled Zoroaster. Nevertheless,

A modern Zoroastrian priest reads from the sacred texts while carefully preparing the haoma *ritual.*

Persians continued to sacrifice animals and to drink *haoma* during Zoroaster's time and long after.

Although the Persians performed animal sacrifices, they did not conduct these rituals thoughtlessly. Killing any valuable beast was no small matter to them. The ancient Persians respected animals, and they not only prayed for the sacrificial beast but even said a prayer for any game they killed when they went hunting. However, they believed that sacrifices were necessary and beneficial. The ceremonies brought them the favor of the gods. In addition the Persians believed that the souls of the dead animals would rise to heaven. There they would join and strengthen the Soul of the Bull, a divinity that protected all animals on earth.

Protecting the Sacred Earth and Air

Besides honoring water and fire, the Persians took great care to protect the earth and the air, more creations of Ahura-Mazda. To avoid polluting the soil, garbage was divided into three groups and eliminated in three different ways: human and animal wastes were used as fertilizers; garbage that could neither enrich nor harm the soil—broken pottery, for example—was buried in rocky sites; everything else was taken to a small stone building and dropped onto a pile through a chimneylike opening on top of the building. Acid was poured down the chimney from time to time to destroy the garbage below. Waste materials were *never* burned, for they polluted fire and air.

It was also forbidden to bury or burn a human corpse. The ancient Persians believed that people died when demons replaced the good spirits that sustained life. Therefore, a corpse was full of evil spirits. If buried, its flesh would pollute the soil; if burned, not only would the sacred flames be polluted, but the demons would be released into the air to do more harm. In fact to bury or burn a corpse was considered a serious offense—so serious that it was punishable by death.

To dispose of the dead, the Persians chose one of two methods. The older method was to put the corpse into underground stone shafts, where the decaying flesh could never come into contact with soil. The second method, which became more popular around Zoroaster's time, was to place the corpse on a stone platform, where the body was exposed to scavengers like vultures who would eat the flesh—and destroy the evil spirits. When the bones had been picked clean, they were left in the sun to dry and purify before being buried in a rocky bed.

Visitors to the cliffs at Naqsh-i-Rustam, near Persepolis in southwestern Iran, can still see the great rock tombs of the Achaemenid kings Artaxerxes I, Xerxes I, and Darius I.

The only exceptions made to these burial practices occurred when kings died. Persian kings were embalmed to preserve their bodies, and their corpses were placed in tombs in rocky cliffs. Here again, the bodies would never come in contact with the soil, and part of the king's spirit, Persians believed, would remain with his body and help his people.

Helping Departed Souls

Several rituals were observed to show respect for the deceased, to strengthen his or her soul for its trip to heaven, and to sustain the soul in paradise until it became fully adjusted to its new surroundings. To give the soul strength to cross the Chinvat bridge, the path to paradise, the survivors mourned for three days, the time a soul was expected to remain on earth. During this time, the deceased's family fasted, prayed, and offered a blood sacrifice. Other sacrifices were made thirty days later, to further strengthen the soul, and at the end of the year, when it was believed that all souls returned to their homes on earth for one night. This journey, too, required nourishment. After the first year, an annual offering was made for thirty years to show respect. These offerings were made by the oldest son of the deceased.

Portraying the Gods in Works of Art

As in other societies, the Persians' religious beliefs were expressed in their works of art. The earliest Persians did not have temples, but they did have small statues of their gods, especially Anahita, the fertility goddess, and Haoma, the god of immortality. These statues were easy to carry around as the nomads moved from place to place.

During the Achaemenian period, the Persians continued to make the small statues, but also began to create larger works of art. They chiseled symbols and figures of their deities into stone for all to see. Stone carvings in such places as Persepolis and the cliffs of Behistun picture Ahura-Mazda, who is often shown as a winged deity, and Mithra, who usually wears a halo of spiky rays of sunshine. Often these gods appear to be blessing the kings. Mythical animals from Mount Alburz were also used as statues, and winged

RELIGIOUS FESTIVALS

Zoroastrians held seven religious festivals each year: the Feast of Midspring; the Feast of Midsummer; the Feast of Bringing in the Corn; the Feast of Homecoming, when cattle were brought in from summer pastures; the Feast of Midwinter; the Feast to Celebrate the Last Night of the Year, the last night of winter on a modern calendar; and New Day, the first day of spring. Because several of these feasts are so closely tied to agricultural life, most historians believe that at least some of these celebrations existed long before Zoroaster began to preach. He simply gave religious meaning to them.

Zoroastrian festivals were daylong celebrations. Believers began by attending religious services to worship Ahura-Mazda. Then congregations gathered around tables near the worship site. These tables were piled high with food, where all members, rich and poor, ate and celebrated together for the rest of the day. The festival, a time of goodwill, was eagerly anticipated by all.

bulls and *simurghs* were pictured in Persian carpets, wall decorations, and silver plates as well.

The stone carvings reminded the ancient Persians of their gods and of the help the gods had given in the past. In addition, the text written below the illustrations told them that the kings ruled because Ahura-Mazda wanted them to do so. For example, on the stone cliffs near Naqsh-i-Rustam (NAK-she-ROO-stahm) Darius ordered the following message to be written: "A great God is Ahura-Mazda, who created this earth, who created yonder sky, who created man . . . who made Darius king, one king over many. . . . He made me king. I am king." Such messages encouraged the Persians to be loyal to their rulers as part of their religious faith and promised political stability—a major effect of the Persian's religious beliefs.

In this beautiful sculpture from his capital of Persepolis, Darius I appears with kingly grace and power. He sits on a high, cushioned throne with his feet on a stool. His robe is richly pleated, and he holds a staff and flower, traditional symbols of royal power in ancient Iran.

CHAPTER FIVE

GIFTS TO HUMANITY

The ancient Persians' historical importance and their gifts to humanity have sometimes been forgotten. Far too often their accomplishments have been overshadowed by those of the Greeks and Romans. This is especially true in the West, where Persian achievements in architecture and art, literature and language, science, and religion receive little credit.

Iwans, Courtyards, and Domes

In architecture, especially, the Persians have left a great legacy. First of all, the ruins at Persepolis and Susa are beautiful to behold, even if they are a mere fragment of what once existed. They are a testament to the Persians' skills, and they are a source of information about the building techniques of many people of the empire as well.

Second, Persian architecture was copied by the Arabs and, later, by other Muslim peoples. They used Persian ideas to create buildings of great beauty throughout their empire, spreading Persian influence over a wide area. The Arabs, for example, greatly admired the Persian invention of the *iwan,* a hallway with a vaulted ceiling, and they copied it often. In mosques, or Muslim

The use of domes in the architecture of the Muslim world can be traced to the technology of the ancient Persians. This especially fine example (center) is the dome of the Blue Mosque in Istanbul, Turkey.

places of worship, *iwans* often served as classrooms during hot summer months. In both their mosques and their houses, the Arabs also used the Persian design of a central courtyard with a formal garden. The garden was a long narrow plot divided into four parts. In the center was a pool.

The Persian courtyard served as a model for other Muslim societies as well. Islamic rulers in India adopted the layout and used it extensively in their country for many years. Some of these gardens are still in existence. One of the most famous sites modeled after the Persian plan is the formal garden at the Taj Mahal in Agra.

Another Persian architectural feature—the dome—was much admired by the Arabs. During the Sasanian period, the Persians had learned how to vary the form of the *iwan* to make a dome. They carefully shaped bricks and mortar into a support, called a squinch, which they placed on the top of a square room to hold a dome. The Persians placed domes only on important buildings, such as a king's palace. The oldest surviving example in Iran today is located at Qaleh-I-Dokhtar (KAL-ah-EE-DOK-tar) on top of King Ardashir's palace. The Arabs placed domes on their most important buildings, too, especially their mosques.

Stone Carvings, Keys to the Past

The ancient Persians have left another legacy to the modern world in their stone carvings. Beautiful works of art were carved on the tombs of kings and on buildings in Persepolis, as well as on the Behistun cliffs. These carvings are not only valuable for their artistry, but also for the information they provide about life in the Persian Empire. They show us what the various people of the empire looked like and how they dressed. They give us a good idea of what kinds of crops and animals were raised. The writings, or inscriptions, below the images describe victories and defeats. Together, the illustrations and messages are "pages" in a unique history book.

Words to Remember

The Persians recorded only a few myths and legends on their rocky cliffs. Today, however, we still can read many of their stories.

Several tales were passed down orally and recorded later. The *Shahnamah (Book of Kings)*—an epic poem some fifty thousand lines long—was written down by a great Persian poet, Firdausi, in the tenth century C.E. The stories of kings, gods, and demons contained in the *Shahnamah* have their origin in ancient Persia. The *Shahnamah* was very popular, and it was printed many times in later years. Some of the first editions were illustrated with miniature paintings, each one done by hand. These were so beautifully painted that they became collectors' items and can be found today in museums throughout the world. The *Shahnamah*, or at least portions of it, can be found in most libraries today.

Another work, the Zend-Avesta, although meant primarily as

The reliefs at Persepolis showing tributaries bringing riches to the Achaemenid kings are very careful to show the differences among the various peoples of the empire. For example, the Phoenician tributaries in the lowest row wear delicately pleated linen clothes, and carry fine metal vessels and finely folded cloth. The Median tributaries above them, however, wear stiffer clothing of thick cloth or leather, and carry bulky cloth and jewelry.

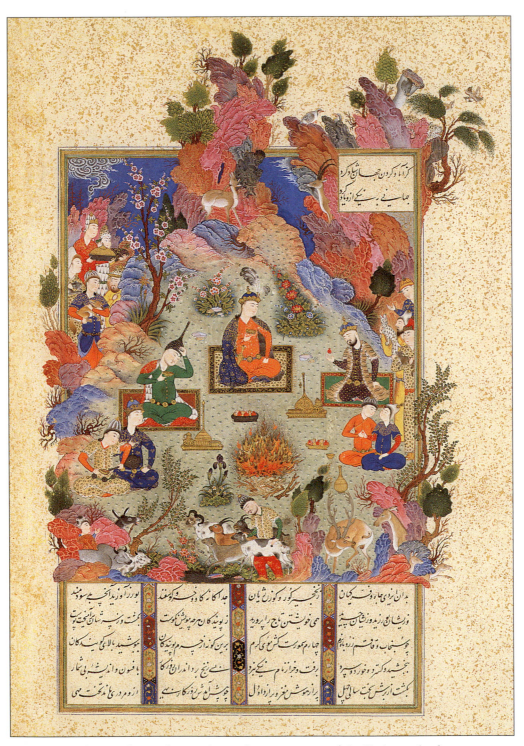

A colorfully illustrated page from a sixteenth-century copy of the Shahnamah, *the great Persian poem. This page shows a sumptuous royal feast in a palace garden.*

a book of faith, was also a major contribution to world literature. Besides myths and legends, it contains beautifully written prose and poetry, hymns, and chants that were said almost three thousand years ago.

Ancient Persian literary characters and mythical animals live on in a variety of art forms. *Simurghs* and dragons and heroic kings have been—and continue to be—portrayed on carpets, murals, silver dishes, and pieces of pottery.

Besides creating characters in stories that would live for more than two thousand years, the ancient Persians passed on vocabulary words to many languages. English contains more than 150 of these, including *bazaar, lemon, magic*, which came from the word *magi, orange, paradise*, and *sherbet*. The phrase *Parthian shot*—which once meant the specific bow-and-arrow feat the Parthians invented—shooting over one's shoulder while riding away from an enemy—has become part of our language. Today it is used to mean a sharp remark made over one's shoulder while walking away from an argument.

Advances in Science, Math, and Agriculture

The Persians also made numerous contributions to the world of science. Their accomplishments resulted mostly from the fact that they allowed people to study, explore, and experiment. This attitude was not typical of the times, for many rulers outlawed scientific exploration, especially if it conflicted with accepted religious beliefs.

Some of the greatest scientific advances were made by the Babylonian astronomer Nabu-rimanni in the fifth century B.C.E. Working in the Persian royal court, Nabu-rimanni made accurate predictions of lunar and solar eclipses. He also plotted the moon's phases and the varying length of the days throughout the year, so that daily variations in sunlight might be anticipated. His work was extremely accurate, and few changes were made in his predictions for more than three hundred years.

Nabu-rimanni was not alone in his quest for knowledge. Other scientists throughout the empire studied astronomy, and mathematicians made great advances in geometry. The reputation

CRACKING THE CODE AT BEHISTUN

In 1835, Major Henry Rawlinson, who was a British military adviser to Kurdistan, one of the Persian provinces, stared in awe at the magnificent carvings at Behistun. However, his awe quickly turned to frustration when he studied the script chiseled into the stone beneath the carvings. A classical scholar and a student of languages, Rawlinson couldn't make sense of even one wedge-shaped mark on the wall. Intrigued by what the script might say, Rawlinson vowed to crack the code.

The major began this challenging project by making copies of the inscriptions on the cliff whenever he could get away from his official duties. Because the carvings were located more than three hundred feet above the base of the cliff, they were difficult to read from the road. To better see the symbols and make an exact copy, Rawlinson scaled the sheer cliff. The message was nearly a thousand lines long, and it took him more than twelve years to complete his task.

Next, Rawlinson had to make sense of what he had copied. He quickly realized that the message had been written in three different languages, Old Persian, Elamite, and Akkadian. Rawlinson decided to tackle Old Persian first, since he recognized, from certain words, similarities to the modern Persian language. He studied the mysterious marks carefully, using trial and error to determine what a mark meant, until he could identify forty Old Persian symbols and the sound each represented.

The lengthy inscription of Darius appears on the cliffs below the sculpted scene at Behistun.

Rawlinson and others then went to work on the Elamite and Akkadian messages, using Old Persian as a guide. It was a slow, tedious task, but by 1857 these, too, could be understood. The scholars' work enabled historians to read some ancient manuscripts and inscriptions that couldn't be translated before, not only in Persia but in many parts of its ancient empire as well. One of the most exciting discoveries made was finding information about the Sumerians, an ancient people in Mesopotamia previously unknown to historians.

of these scholars spread, and scientists from all over the ancient world came to the Persian Empire to increase their knowledge. The visitors took information back to their homelands, added the new learning to what had already been discovered, and created a vast body of knowledge that is still studied today.

The ancient Persians also left a lasting legacy in farming and gardening. They introduced new crops, such as barley and rice, to countries in their empire. The new crops flourished and continued to be raised long after the Persians lost their empire. The Persians' love of flowers, especially those with rich, heavy fragrances, led them to transplant species growing in the wild into their own gardens. They domesticated vari-

DAMASK ROSE

Damask roses, among the most fragrant of all roses, grew wild in ancient Persia. Persians transplanted them to their gardens, where they could enjoy the flowers close up.

There are several stories about how these roses spread throughout Europe and then to North America. The most likely account claims that Roman soldiers couldn't help noticing roses when they invaded Persia, and they brought plants back to Italy. Later the Romans took roses to a variety of places in their empire, including England. Roses were probably transported across the ocean to North America by English colonists.

eties of wild irises, lilacs, and roses. Visitors took seeds and roots from some of these varieties to other parts of the world, where they have been cultivated for many centuries. Descendants of ancient varieties can be found all over the world today.

As avid gardeners and farmers, the Persians were well aware that good soil and clean water were precious. One of their greatest

PERSIAN CARPETS TODAY

Unfortunately, few rugs from the Achaemenians' time exist today, for carpets, unlike stone statues, rarely survive for thousands of years. The best-known example of an ancient Persian rug, believed to be the oldest, is in a museum in St. Petersburg, Russia. It was found in a tomb in Siberia and it is thought to be about 2,500 years old.

In fact most of the oldest carpets now in existence were made in the fifteenth and sixteenth centuries. However, because Persian rug makers continued to use ancient techniques, and similar fabrics, dyes, and designs for hundreds of years after the Persian Empire ended, these rugs are thought to be very much like those the ancients made. As a result, Persian carpets from this era are in great demand today. Museums around the world want to add them to their collections, and private collectors seek these carpets to adorn their homes. But because such rugs are rare and very expensive—some are valued at $200,000—only the wealthiest people can afford them.

Therefore, most people who want Persian carpets today purchase new rugs from sources in Iran. Modern Persian carpets are made in twelve rug-making centers scattered throughout the country. Although all use ancient patterns, each area produces its own unique style. Experts can tell where a rug was made by examining its design, colors, materials, and the methods used to make it.

legacies was their ability to pass on to the next generation a clean environment.

Ideas That Live On

The greatest Persian legacy, according to some historians, may have been Zoroaster's influence on other religions. Zoroaster's idea of personal salvation—that men and women could choose to do good or evil and thereby go to heaven or hell as a result—is still believed by many people today. Although not all religions accept this concept, almost all expect followers to do good works as an outward sign of their faith.

The Zoroastrians were also the first to believe in guardian

ZOROASTRIANISM TODAY

Unable to practice Zoroastrianism once the Arabs had conquered the Persian Empire, some of Zoroaster's followers fled the empire, settling primarily in India. Holding firm to their traditions, they did not modify their beliefs, nor would they accept converts.

Over the next fifteen hundred years, Zoroastrians settled in Pakistan, Sri Lanka (Ceylon), Great Britain, Canada, the United States, Australia, Hong Kong, Singapore, and China. Some followers eventually moved to Iran, bringing the faith back to the land where it began.

angels, a final judgment day, and a resurrection day, when bodies and souls will be miraculously reunited. Many people believe in at least one of these ideas today.

Some Zoroastrian practices—for example the drinking of wine or *haoma* to symbolize union with a god who died and was reborn—are similar to rites in other faiths. Whether the ancient Persians originated these practices is not certain, for clearly they gathered many ideas from other peoples.

And finally, a popular ancient Persian religious festival is still celebrated, in a somewhat different form, today. The Persians held a festival on the shortest day of the year. It was in honor of Mithra, the sun god, who they knew would soon bring them longer days. This holiday spread throughout the empire. It was even celebrated by Roman soldiers who joined Mithra's followers and, in turn,

brought the holiday to the Roman Empire. Christians, unsure of the exact day of Christ's birth, chose to celebrate his birthday at the same time, and the day eventually became known not as Mithra's Day but as Christmas Day, a truly lasting legacy.

According to the Christian story, three ancient Persian magi were among the first to carry gifts to the infant Christ. This scene of the Adoration of the Magi was painted by the Italian artist Sandro Botticelli in the fifteenth century.

71

The Persian Empire: A Time Line

B.C.E.
2000   **1800**   **c. 1000**

B.C.E.

2000-1800 (?)

Aryans (Medes and Persians) migrate to the area now known as Iran

c. 1000

Birth of Zoroaster

c. 560

Cyrus begins his reign

550

Persians conquer the Medes

547

Persians conquer Lydia

529

Cambyses begins his reign

525

Cambyses invades and conquers Egypt

522

Cambyses dies and Darius takes command

513

Darius invades Europe

486

Xerxes becomes ruler of Persian Empire

480

Xerxes invades Greece

465

Xerxes is assassinated, and a struggle over the Persian throne begins

330

Alexander the Great conquers Persepolis

C.E.

c. 560   330   171   53   224   642

171

Parthians begin to take
parts of the empire
from the Greeks

C.E.

53

Parthians defeat the Romans
at Carrhae

C.E.

224

Sasanians take control of
Persian Empire

642

Arabs conquer
the Sasanians

GLOSSARY

alfalfa: a plant with bluish purple flowers grown as a food for cattle, horses, and other livestock

archaeologist: a scientist who studies ancient civilizations by excavating their ruins and examining the remains, such as weapons, pottery, and tools

astronomer: a scientist who studies stars and planets, their motions and positions

capital: top part of a column or pillar

citrus fruits: juicy fruits with thick rinds, such as lemons, limes, oranges, and grapefruit

cuneiform: a system of writing developed around 3000 B.C.E. in Mesopotamia in which wedge-shaped symbols were used to represent sounds

deity: a god or goddess

demon: a spirit, usually evil but sometimes a force for good

limestone: a soft stone, usually white, easily cut and carved; not as durable as granite or marble

mail: flexible armor of interlinked metal rings fashioned into coats for warriors to wear in battle

mosque: a Muslim place of worship

Muslims: followers of Muhammad, who founded the religion of Islam in the seventh century C.E. Muslims believe that there is one god, Allah, and that Muhammad is his prophet.

oasis: a place in a desert where trees, shrubs, and other plants can grow because there is a supply of water

pomegranate: a round red fruit with a tough skin, a juicy red pulp, and many seeds; grows on trees in warm climates

qanats: canals that channeled water from the mountains in ancient Persia to people's homes

scriptures: a group of writings or a book considered sacred; the Bible or the Zoroastrian Book of Knowledge are examples

seminomadic tribe: a group of people who live in temporary homes and move from season to season but have a base camp at which some crops are grown

tambourine: a musical instrument made of a wooden hoop with a skin stretched over it. Pairs of metal disks are connected to the hoop, which is played by shaking the frame or striking the skin.

tunic: a simple slip-on garment made with or without sleeves. Usually worn knee-length or longer, it was often belted at the waist. Tunics were worn by both men and women in ancient Greece and Rome as well as in ancient Persia.

FOR FURTHER READING

Collins, Robert. *The Medes and Persians: Conquerors and Diplomats*. New York: McGraw-Hill, 1972.

Feinstein, Alan S. *Folk Tales from Persia*. South Brunswick, New Jersey: A. S. Barnes, 1971.

Ghirshman, Roman, Vladimir Minorsky, and Ramesh Sanghvi. *Persia, the Immortal Kingdom*. New York: New York Graphic Society, 1971.

Harris, Nathaniel. *Rugs and Carpets of the Orient*. London: Hamlyn, 1977.

Hinnells, John R. *Persian Mythology*. London: Hamlyn House, 1973.

Osborne, Christine. *Middle Eastern Food and Drink*. New York: Bookwright Press, 1988.

Picard, Barbara Leonie. *Tales of Ancient Persia*. New York: Henry Z. Walck, 1972.

Esther. This Old Testament book, written by Esther's guardian, Mordeci, is the story of Xerxes's queen, a Jew by the name of Esther. Besides giving interesting details about court life in Persia, it tells how Esther saved her people from slaughter, an event celebrated each year on Purim, a special Jewish holiday. Most libraries carry copies of the Old Testament, which called Xerxes Ahasuerus. Younger readers may wish to use modern revised editions.

BIBLIOGRAPHY

Boyce, Mary. *Zoroastrians: Their Religious Beliefs and Practices.* Boston: Routledge & Kegan Paul, 1979.

Campbell, Joseph. *The Masks of God: Oriental Mythology.* New York: Viking Press, 1962.

Durrant, Will. *Our Oriental Heritage.* New York: Simon & Schuster, 1954.

Eliot, Alexander. *Myths.* New York: McGraw-Hill, 1979.

Ghirshman, Roman, Vladimir Minorsky, and Ramesh Sanghvi. *Persia, the Immortal Kingdom.* New York: New York Graphic Society, 1971.

Harris, Nathaniel. *Rugs and Carpets of the Orient.* London: Hamlyn, 1977.

Hick, Jim. *The Emergence of Man: The Persians.* New York: Time-Life Books, 1975.

Hinnells, John R. *Persian Mythology.* London: Hamlyn House, 1973.

Irving, Clive. *Crossroads of Civilization: 3000 Years of Persian History.* New York: Harper & Row, 1979.

Schoeps, Hans-Joachim. *The Religions of Mankind.* Garden City, New York: Doubleday, 1966.

Titley, Norah, and Frances Wood. *Oriental Gardens: An Illustrated History.* San Francisco: Chronicle Books, 1991.

INDEX

Page numbers for illustrations are in boldface

ABOUT THE AUTHOR

Karen Zeinert is the author of eight books for young people, including the award-winning *The Warsaw Ghetto Uprising*. Her work has also appeared in children's magazines, such as *Cricket* and *Cobblestone*. *The Persian Empire* is her first book for Marshall Cavendish.

A former social studies teacher, who holds degrees in history and English, Ms. Zeinert enjoys studying the past and its influence on the present. The ancient Persians are of special interest to her, not only because of their remarkable military accomplishments, but also because of their love of gardening—Zeinert is an avid gardener—and their commitment to protect their natural resources.

Ms. Zeinert and her husband, John, a former history teacher, live in a woods near Neenah, Wisconsin, where many forms of wildlife—birds, deer, squirrels, raccoons, and even a coyote or two—thrive. The Zeinerts like to travel, and they enjoy visiting gardens and historic sites in the United States and abroad.